AF585261

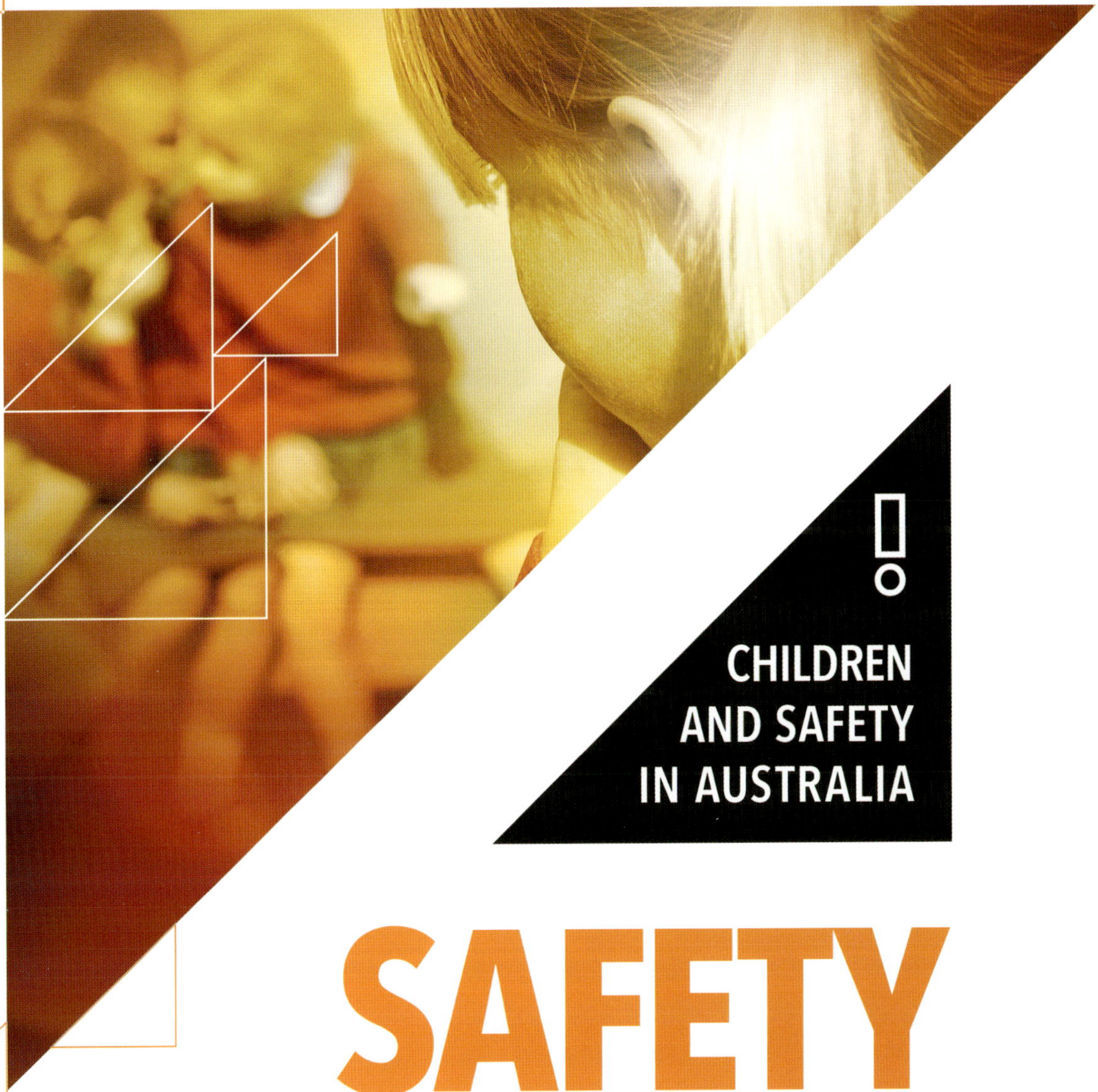

CHILDREN AND SAFETY IN AUSTRALIA

SAFETY AT SCHOOL

WILLIAM DAY

Redback Publishing
PO Box 357 Frenchs Forest NSW 2086
Australia

www.redbackpublishing.com.au
orders@redbackpublishing.com.au

978-1-925630-67-1

Author: William Day
Editor: Marianne Lindsell
Designer: Redback Publishing

Original illustrations © Redback Publishing 2018
Originated by Redback Publishing

Printed and bound in China by Leo Paper

MIX
Paper from responsible sources
FSC® C020056

Acknowledgements
Abbreviations: l—left, r—right, b—bottom, t—top, c—centre, m—middle
We would like to thank the following for permission to reproduce photographs:
(Images © shutterstock)

Every effort has been made to contact copyright holders of any material reproduced in this book. Any omissions will be rectified in subsequent printings if notice is given to the publisher.

A catalogue record for this book is available from the National Library of Australia

CONTENTS

INTRODUCTION

School is a place where children should be able to feel completely safe and happy. There are many things that can interfere with the safety of a child at school, ranging from dangerous parts of buildings, to harmful acts by other people.

Children and adults can lessen these threats to safety by being aware of what they are, and then knowing what actions they can take to reduce the dangers, or remove them altogether.

FEELING UNSAFE

There's nothing wrong with feeling unsafe and scared. Being scared means that you are sensible enough to know that there is danger around. Being scared is not your fault and you have a right not to feel that way.

Older children at school can play an important role by looking after the safety of younger students. Every child can try to be aware of dangers at school, and then inform teachers or trusted adults if they see anything that might cause harm to other students.

UNICEF's Convention on the Rights of the Child (CRC)

Australia agreed to the principles of the CRC in 1980. The only two United Nations members which do not fully agree with the CRC are the USA and Somalia. There are 54 Articles in the CRC.

Here are three of the 54 CRC Articles that apply to safety at school:

Article 19
Governments should ensure that children are properly cared for and protect them from violence, abuse and neglect by their parents, or anyone else who looks after them.

Article 28
Children have the right to an education. Discipline in schools should respect children's human dignity.

Article 29
Education should develop each child's personality and talents to the full. It should encourage children to respect their parents, their cultures and other cultures.

Who Makes School Rules?

Every school has safety rules and regulations. Even if you sometimes don't want to keep to the rules, try to remember that they have been created to keep children and adults safe.

When you leave primary school, and become a teenager and later an adult, you will find that there are many rules for people living in Australia. Rules for adults include laws made by governments. Breaking these laws can be a serious criminal offence, and involve fines or time spent in jail.

People who are at least 18 years old can vote for the people they want to represent them in Australia's parliaments. These elected representatives then make the laws that govern everyone in Australia. At school, some rules are made by the government, and others are made by the Principal, teachers and parents. If your school has elected class captains, or a student council, then you might have experience in electing one student to represent your whole class.

BULLYING

Bullying includes many different sorts of actions

Physical bullying involves children harming each other with violent behaviour.

Psychological bullying involves trying to make another child feel sad and unhappy.

Social bullying involves excluding a child from groups or not talking to them.

Online bullying involves using phones or social media to upset someone.

Schools in Australia have plans for dealing with bullying. Talk about it with your parent, trusted adult or teacher. Trying to keep bullying a secret only makes you feel worse. You don't need to feel guilty because other people are bullying you.

What if you are the bully?

Do you sometimes feel that you need to bully someone else because your group of friends is doing it? Part of growing up means that you learn to judge what is right and what is wrong. Doing something wrong just because other people want you to is not the right way to live your life.

CHILD ABUSE AND NEGLECT

All the states and territories in Australia have laws that require teachers to report to the relevant government body if they suspect a child is being abused or neglected. This is called Mandatory Reporting.

If you feel very upset because of something serious that is happening to you, talk to a teacher you trust. They may be able to help you, or find someone else who can.

Stop

KIDS HELPLINE
Phone 1800 55 1800

Send an email to counsellor@kidshelpline.com.au or chat online at their website www.kidshelpline.com.au

Free for young people from 5 to 25 years old in Australia

PLAYGROUNDS

The school playground could have out-of-bounds areas where you are not allowed to go. These areas may be unsafe because they are isolated and teachers cannot see if there is any danger there. There may also be dangerous buildings that need repair.

Some playgrounds are a shared zone where children walk and cars or trucks drive into the grounds as well. Being in these areas at times when they are out-of-bounds can result in an accident happening. If you are playing with a ball and throw it into an area where children are not supposed to be, you could be in danger if you try to go and collect it. Ask a teacher for permission first.

Schools that are renewing their playground equipment may place signs around the area to tell children to stay away. Never try to sneak onto unsafe playgrounds equipment, as it could fall over and injure you.

If you see something in the playground that should not be there, tell a teacher so they can find out if there is any danger.

SPORTS FIELDS

If your school is fortunate enough to have a sports field, there are probably rules about how and when you can use it. These rules exist for important reasons.

The grass on the sports field, whether it is real or synthetic, needs protection so that it provides a good surface for teams when they play their matches. Never leave anything sharp or dirty there.

Everyone needs to share the sports field, so let teams play their match before walking across the field and getting in the players' way. You could also be hit by a ball during a match, as the players will not expect someone who is not part of either team to suddenly appear in the middle of the field.

FOOD AT SCHOOL

Tips for keeping your lunch and snacks safe to eat at school

- Keep your lunch in the shade or preferably inside where it will not get warm.
- Add a small ice-pack to keep your food safe to eat.
- Milk and meat will start to deteriorate very quickly if they are kept in a warm place.
- If anything in your lunch smells, looks or tastes bad, don't eat it.
- Wash your hands before eating.
- Don't eat unwrapped food that has flies sitting on it or that has fallen on the ground.

Allergies

There are more children with food allergies in Australia than ever before. Some scientists believe this may be a result of the poisons and pollution which are all around us.

GROAN!
If you have a milk allergy, have you ever asked this question?

YOU: I'm allergic to milk. Do you have any soy drink instead?
THEM: No, but we have skim milk.

What is wrong with this answer?

If you are allergic to some foods, such as nuts, dairy, eggs or anything else, don't share food with other children. You will also have to be extra careful if there is a fete or cake stall at school. There could be ingredients in that delicious-looking biscuit that will make you very sick. Children with allergies will be used to others not understanding how dangerous it can be to offer them food with an ingredient that can result in them having an allergic reaction to it. They will also know that they should always have their Epipen with them at school.

SCHOOL KITCHENS

Safety rules when using school kitchens during cooking classes

- Keep your hands clean.
- Kitchen utensils are not toys. Don't play games with them.
- Don't run in the kitchen.
- Take care with hot foods and with stoves.
- Raw meat should not be on the same surface or plate as cooked meat or vegetables.
- When mixing dry ingredients and liquids, such as milk and flour, add the liquid to the flour, not the other way around. This stops a cloud of flour coming out of the mixing bowl.
- Share the space and utensils with others. Take care not to turn around suddenly when you are holding knives or bowls of food.
- Never add liquid to hot oil as this will cause the oil to splatter everywhere. Hot oil sometimes does not have any bubbles in it, so it may be difficult to tell if it is hot just by looking at it.
- Wear safe shoes. Even professional chefs must wear safety shoes in their kitchens.

SCIENCE LAB

Children who love science enjoy being allowed to use the scientific equipment in the science laboratory. They can pretend they are real scientists!

Scientists have lots of rules for using chemicals and equipment in the laboratory. These rules have been developed over hundreds of years and are designed to keep people safe. The rules also ensure that the results of experiments are not ruined by using careless procedures.

Safety in the Science Lab

- ✓ Use safety goggles when experimenting.
- ✓ Use a fume cupboard to do experiments that release dangerous or unpleasant gases.
- ✓ Take care with Bunsen burners.
- ✓ Never run, sit on the bench or play games in a science lab.
- ✓ Don't eat or drink in the science lab.
- ✓ Follow safety rules when using chemicals. Substances that start out being harmless can become dangerous during the course of a chemistry experiment.

FIRST AID COURSES FOR CHILDREN

When an accident occurs, it can take a while for emergency services to arrive. Everyone can learn first aid, even children, so that they can help out before the professionals arrive.

RED CROSS

The Red Cross in Australia runs first aid courses for children. The courses are for children aged 8 to 11. They can learn the basics of first aid and may be able to use these skills to save a life or at least to make an injured person feel more comfortable. The subjects covered include what to do if someone is unconscious, bleeding, has been poisoned, received an electric shock or a burn, or has something stuck in their eye, ear or nose.

ST JOHN AMBULANCE

The First Aid in Schools Program from St John Ambulance is for children in primary school. Young students learn the first aid skills they will need to make them confident to help if there is an emergency. The courses are held either in schools or online.

ROYAL LIFE SAVING SOCIETY AUSTRALIA

The first aid courses run by the Royal Life Saving Society are for people from 14 years old. Students learn about the theory behind first aid, including how the body works and why first aid is important. Students also learn practical skills, such as resuscitation, using bandages and how to apply first aid to a broken limb.

The Bronze Medallion is a lifesaving qualification that means a person has learned to perform basic water rescues. The course for this award is open to people from 14 years and older. The Bronze Medallion is the minimum qualification required by a lifesaver. Students learn resuscitation, how to tow a person in the water, survival and rescue skills, as well as the theory behind being safe in the water.

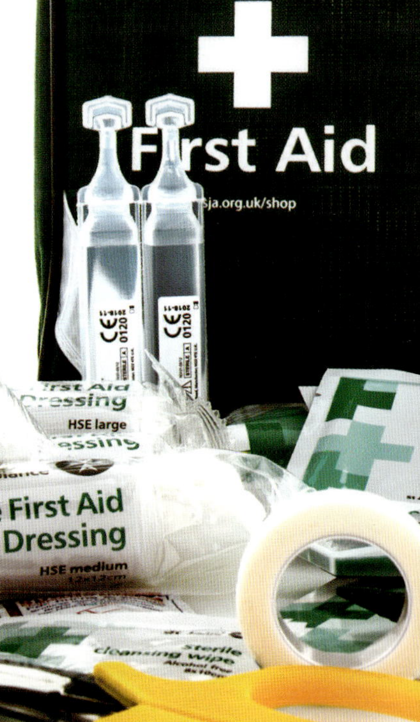

ROADS INSIDE AND OUTSIDE SCHOOLS

Roads Outside Schools

Millions of Australian school students travel to and from school each school day. Here are some tips for keeping safe on or near roads:

- ✓ Even if you are using a pedestrian crossing outside your school, and there is a crossing guard on duty, always look for yourself to make sure cars are going to stop before you cross.
- ✓ The traffic outside schools can be very busy, and this means it is difficult for drivers to see you clearly. Don't dash across the road in front of cars, or move behind a car that may reverse into you. The design of some large, high cars makes it hard for drivers to see if a small child is on the road behind them.
- ✓ Encouraging a friend on the other side of the road to run across to join you is a dangerous thing to do.
- ✓ School children travelling on buses should stay in their seats if they have one, or hold onto a rail if standing. Buses may have to stop suddenly if there is an emergency on the road. When getting off a bus at school, don't run across the road in front of or behind the bus.

Roads Inside Schools

People in delivery trucks sometimes drive inside school grounds. They might not be used to driving there, so take care when you see them in your school. If you are too close to the back of the truck when the driver starts to reverse, you will not be visible in the driving mirrors.

The doors at the back of delivery trucks may swing open sideways and can injure anyone who happens to be walking past. The driver might not know that there are students walking or running near the truck, so take care of your own safety and keep a safe distance away.

SCHOOL GARDENS

Many schools are encouraging students to start vegetable gardens in the school grounds. This is a wonderful way to find out how to grow your own food. You will also discover the names of different sorts of vegetables and fruits, some of which you might not have seen before.

School gardens are a practical way to show children the basics of environmental sustainability, which is included in the Australian Curriculum. Are pesticides really necessary? Can we grow all our food organically, without adding any dangerous chemicals to kill pests? Young gardeners who see the effects of pests on their small crops can discuss the answers to these questions after they have grown food for themselves.

Gardening at school can present the same sorts of hazards as gardening at home. Spiders, biting insects, snakes and sharp garden tools are all dangers that children need to be aware of when they start gardening. Children who are allergic to certain fruits or vegetables should not only avoid eating them but also even touching them if they are growing in the school garden.

SUN SAFETY

Being careful not to get sunburnt is important because too much exposure to the sun can lead to skin cancers in later life. The No Hat No Play rule in schools is there to protect students, even though it seems very annoying when all you want to do is go outside and play.

We need only a few minutes of sun on our skins to help our bodies produce Vitamin D each day. This vitamin is necessary for strong and healthy bones. The sun in the middle part of the day in summer is much more damaging to skin than in the early morning or late afternoon. Try to avoid being in the sun during the hottest part of the day, and use a sunscreen to protect parts of the body that are not covered, like faces and ears.

Too much UV light from the sun can damage our eyes as well as our skin. This is why we need to wear sunglasses. Some inexpensive sunglasses are just as good at protecting our eyes as the most expensive brands.

The Cancer Council of Australia organises the SunSmart Program to help schools around Australia keep their students and teachers safe in the sun.

TOYS AT SCHOOL

Children like to bring their favourite toys to share with their friends at school. If a toy is easily breakable, it is best not to bring it to school, as other people might not know how to handle it safely. You could also cause your friends to become jealous of each other if they all want to play with your toy at the same time.

Toys that shoot hard objects could injure other students, and toys with tiny parts can be a danger to children in preschool or kindergarten. Leave these toys at home. Even if younger children do not play with your toy, you may drop pieces on the ground where a young child could find them later.

Little children love to put tiny pieces of toys in their mouths and may choke on them. Toys with button shaped batteries in them should never be used near very young children, as they may put the battery in their mouth and swallow it. Some children who have done this needed an operation in hospital to remove the battery.

BRINGING MONEY OR JEWELLERY TO SCHOOL

The only money you should take to school is what you really need for the day. You might need to have extra money if there is a book fair or a fete at school. Book fairs often allow parents to prepay online, so all a student needs to bring to school is a receipt number. If you have money at school, keep it in your pocket, or allow the school office to look after it for you. Leaving money in your school bag, where you cannot see it, is not a good idea.

School is not the place to wear expensive jewellery. Adults going to work do not wear their best jewellery, and school is like a workplace for children. Although you may want to show off some jewellery you have just bought or received as a gift, do this on the weekend, not at school.

TAKING CARE OF YOUNGER CHILDREN

A school is a community. Everyone there needs to look after the welfare of each other. Schools usually separate the playground into areas for very young and older children. This helps to keep little children in preschool or kindergarten safe from the boisterous games that older children play. Even if your little sister or brother is in kindergarten, encourage them to play in their own area, rather than coming to find you in the playground. The exception to this might be if your parents and teachers think you need to comfort them, particularly if it is their very first day at school.

If you see a little child who is in the wrong area, is being bullied or who has suffered an injury of some sort, tell a teacher immediately.

In before and after school care, children of all ages may be together in the one area. In these situations, act responsibly so that little children are not frightened or harmed by actions that older children might think are normal for their own age group.

MEDICINES AND FEELING SICK

If you need to bring your medicines or your Epipen to school, let your teachers know so that they realise you have permission from home to have medicines with you. Some medicines need to be kept cool, and some can be harmful if anyone else takes them. Because of this, you may have to leave your medicines in the school office.

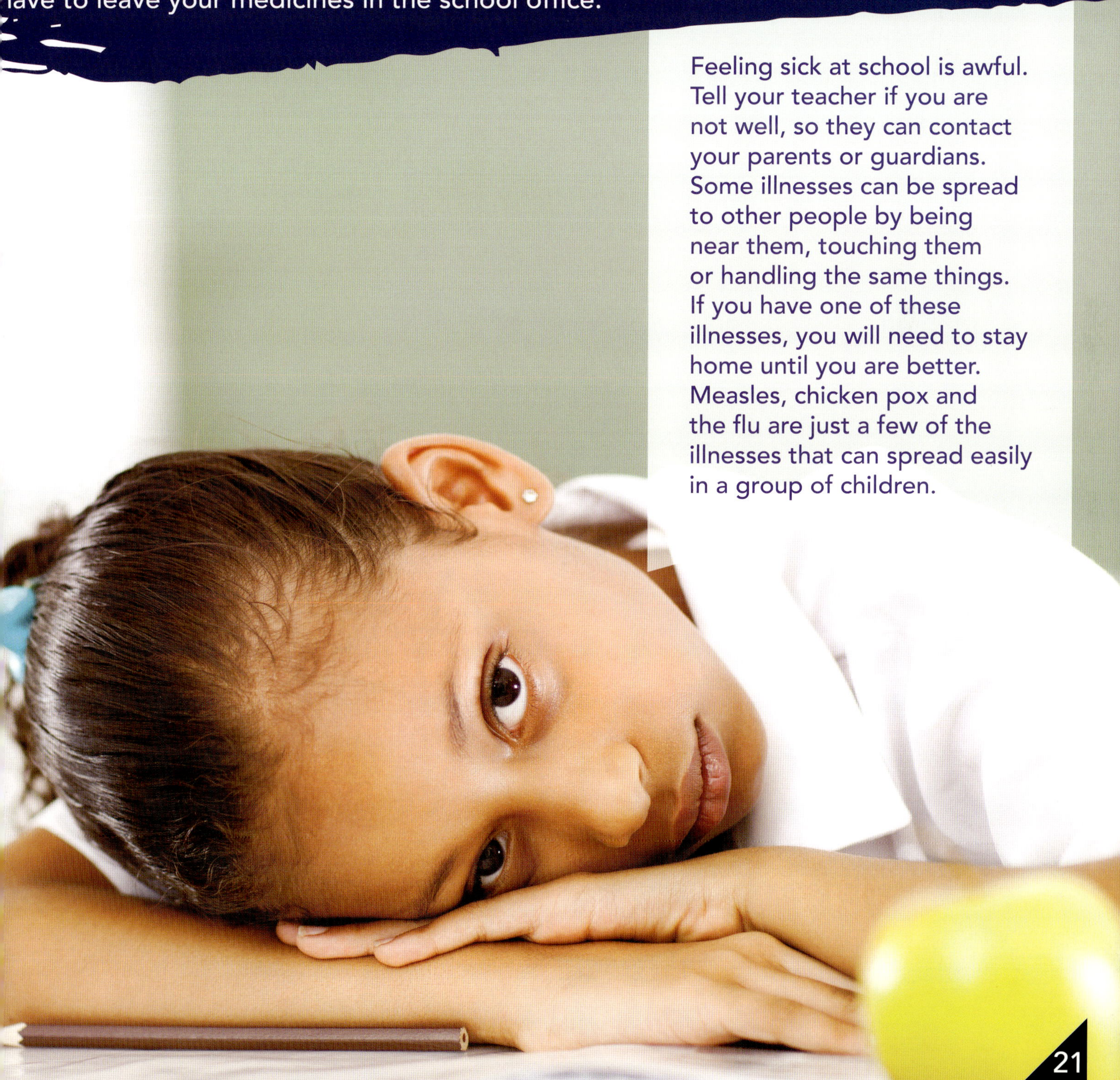

Feeling sick at school is awful. Tell your teacher if you are not well, so they can contact your parents or guardians. Some illnesses can be spread to other people by being near them, touching them or handling the same things. If you have one of these illnesses, you will need to stay home until you are better. Measles, chicken pox and the flu are just a few of the illnesses that can spread easily in a group of children.

SCHOOL EXCURSIONS

School excursions are exciting. Whether you are walking as a group, or travelling in a bus, train or airplane, everyone needs to take a little bit of extra care when they are in a large group on a school excursion.

Walking Excursions

- ✓ When walking along a footpath in a school group, keep away from the kerb.
- ✓ Don't play games that could push another child onto the road.
- ✓ Keep up with the group and be aware of Stranger Danger.

Public Transport

- ✓ Use seatbelts if they are fitted in the vehicle you are in.
- ✓ Keep all parts of your body inside the vehicle and don't hang your hands or arms out windows.
- ✓ Don't run across roads when you get off the bus. Cross together with the group.

General Safety

- ✓ Teachers will mark your name off their list to make sure you are still in the group.
- ✓ Stay with the group.
- ✓ Listen to any special safety instructions from your teacher or other people in charge of the excursion.
- ✓ If you notice someone is missing, tell a teacher.
- ✓ If you feel sick, tell a teacher.

TRAVELLING OVERSEAS

If you are lucky enough to go overseas on a school excursion there are many safety issues you need to be aware of.

Many countries overseas have cultural standards that are different from those in Australia. Noisy, rowdy behaviour may be unacceptable and will cause trouble for you and the group you are with.

Visitors to churches, mosques and temples may need to wear special types of clothing and take off their shoes. Any disrespectful behaviour can result in the whole group being expelled.

Remember that you are representing not only your school but your country when you travel with a group overseas.

Stay with your group and be aware of Stranger Danger.

LOCKDOWNS

Schools in Australia have developed lockdown procedures to deal with emergency situations that involve the whole school.

A lockdown can be announced for a number of different reasons such as:

- There is a dangerous intruder in the school grounds or buildings
- A dangerous storm is coming
- There is a threatening situation near the school
- There are dangerous animals on the grounds

Teachers and staff receive training in what to do during a lockdown, so listen to their instructions. Lockdowns can be very frightening, but they are for your safety. Many schools all around the world have lockdown procedures, so they are not unique to Australia.

Q. & A.

Q. Why do some lockdown notifications involve using music over a loudspeaker?

A. The music is less upsetting for students and for any intruders in the school.

STRANGER DANGER

The rules of Stranger Danger apply at school just as they do anywhere else. Strangers can be people outside the school fence, or people who have come into the school grounds.

Strangers in the school grounds should not talk to students. Most schools have a school office which is easy to find, and any school visitor should talk to the school staff if they need information.

Strangers who are outside the school fence may try to encourage children to come outside by saying that the child's family needs them to leave right away. This could be a lie and the person might be seeking to cause harm.

WHAT WOULD YOU DO?

If a parent or trusted adult usually comes to collect you after school, what would you do if a stranger came instead and said you should leave with them?

NATURAL DISASTERS

Natural disasters in Australia threaten life and property across the country. Schools in areas prone to natural disasters have emergency plans for keeping everyone safe. If a natural disaster might occur, schools can be closed until the emergency is over.

A disaster can happen suddenly, or government organisations sometimes provide warning that an emergency event is about to occur

- ✓ People who study meteorology use their technical resources to work out if a large storm or cyclone is on the way. They can also predict heavy snow storms, heat waves or below freezing temperatures.
- ✓ The Joint Australian Tsunami Warning Centre provides advance information to Australians about tsunamis that will arrive along coastal areas, and which may spread upstream along rivers.
- ✓ Rural fire services notify the daily fire danger ratings.
- ✓ Geoscience Australia has sensors that monitor earthquake activity around Australia. It also keeps track of any earthquakes beyond Australia's borders that might result in tsunamis affecting the coastal areas.

GET READY KIDS

Get Ready Kids is an education program for children from kindergarten to year 9. Compiled by the New South Wales State Emergency Service, the program covers what children can do to stay safe in storms and floods.

EMERGENCY SERVICES IN AUSTRALIA

Emergency Services in Australia are provided by governments and private organisations. Some of the people who work in these services are employees, while others are volunteers.

People who work as police officers, ambulance paramedics or fire fighters often visit schools to talk about what they do. They also show students the technical equipment that modern emergency service workers need to perform their important work.

Emergency service workers are some of the most admired people in our community. They save the lives of people and animals, they protect property and they put their own lives at risk every working day.

POLICE

State and territory governments in Australia provide their own police services.

AMBULANCE

Paramedics train on the job and by undertaking courses.

FIRE AND RESCUE SERVICES

Highly trained fire fighters respond to emergencies and provide information services for members of the public.

RURAL FIRE SERVICES

These services depend on their volunteer fire fighters.

CAREFLIGHT

An air ambulance service that uses the skills of doctors, nurses, paramedics and pilots.

AUSTRALIAN MARITIME SAFETY AUTHORITY

Provides search and rescue services at sea, as well as management of major ocean pollution incidents.

POISONS INFORMATION LINE

Call 13 11 26 from anywhere in Australia.

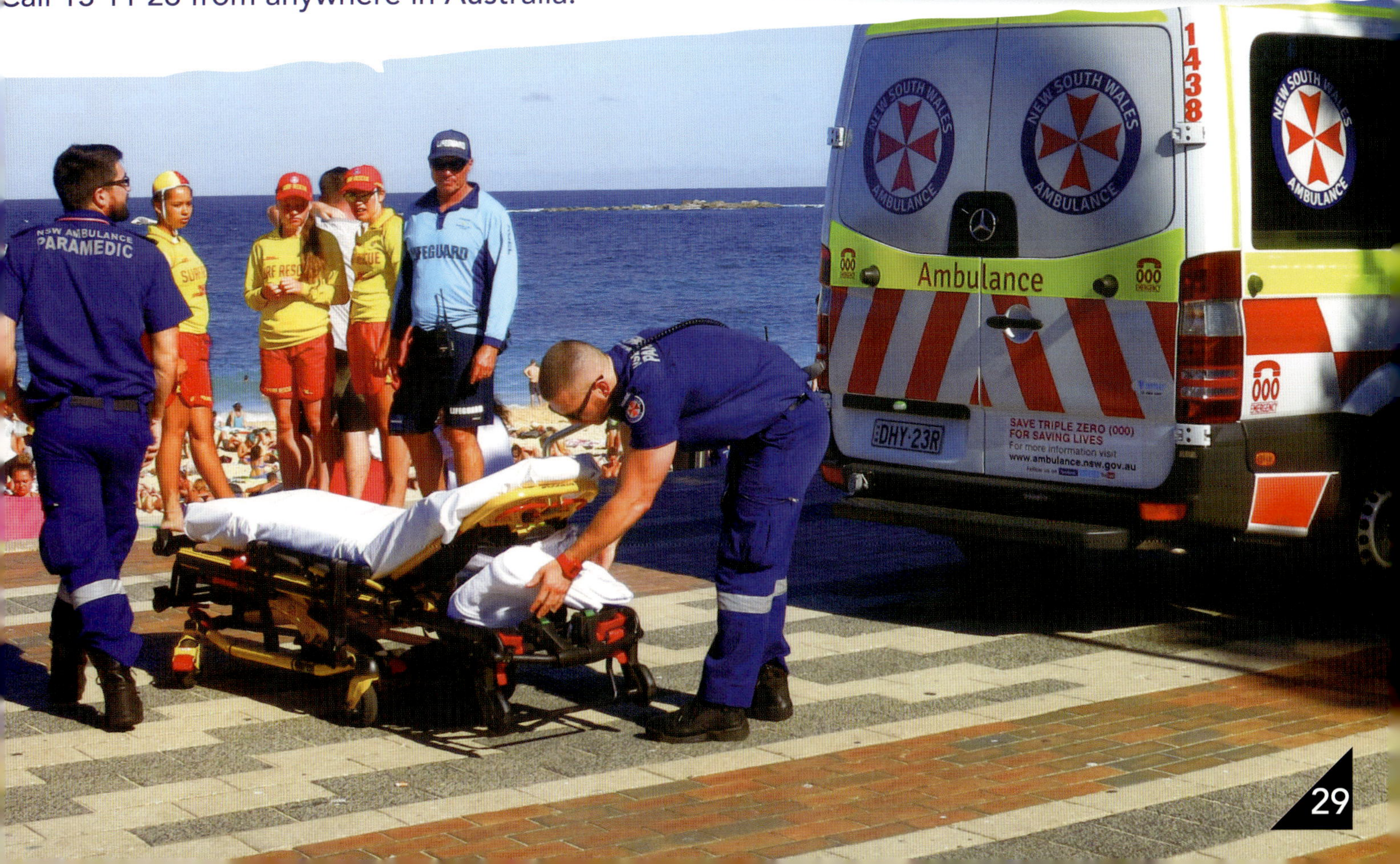

SCHOOL SAFETY AROUND THE WORLD

Schools in countries around the world all have ways to keep their students safe. Here are a few of the ways they do this:

New Zealand
Children learn what to do if there is an earthquake. They practice the three steps of 1. drop to the ground, 2. cover your head, 3. hold on to something in your shelter spot.

Japan
Children with a cold, or those who want to avoid catching one, wear a surgical mask to cover their mouth and nose.

Finland
Finland has nationwide programs to prevent injuries to children playing sport at school.

USA
Lockdowns keep children safe if there is an intruder in the school.

Hawaii, USA
Lava flowing from the Kilauea volcano in 2014 resulted in the closure of local schools.

Beijing, China
The Chinese government encourages schools to check the health of all students every day. This helps prevent the spread of diseases amongst the students.

Fiji
After a tropical cyclone destroyed many schools in Fiji in 2016, the government was determined to ensure that new construction methods would lead to more disaster resistant school buildings.

Canada
The Safe Routes to School program advises parents and children on the correct clothing to wear in snow and below freezing temperatures on their way to school.

Iraq
Children in Iraq know there are unexploded bombs left behind in former war zones. These bombs are a threat to Iraqi children returning to school when conflict ceases.

Zimbabwe
Some school gardens in country areas need electric fences to keep out large wild animals.

Indonesia
Some schools in Indonesia are located in areas that could be affected by a tsunami. The students learn what to do if a tsunami comes while they are at school.

Papua New Guinea
Most of the population of Papua New Guinea lives in rural areas. Children in these areas have to walk long distances to get to school, often on dirt tracks that are likely to be destroyed during periods of high rainfall. Part of the Australian government's aid program to Papua New Guinea is aimed at improving children's education.

GLOSSARY

allergy - illness that happens as a result of exposure to some substances
boisterous - lively and excited
Bunsen burner - gas burning equipment in a science lab
chef - professional person whose occupation is cooking
deteriorate - get worse or decay
Epipen - medical device used by people with severe allergies
fume cupboard - workspace in a science lab that draws gases away through a chimney
mandatory - required by an official regulation or law
meteorology - study of climate and weather
organic food - food grown without pesticides or other chemical additives
psychological - referring to the workings of the mind
resuscitation - reviving an unconscious person
sustainability - keeping and reusing resources to stop them running out
synthetic - created by humans rather than being natural
tsunami - large, destructive wave that flows inland from the sea
unconscious - not aware of or responding to surroundings
utensil - small household tool
UV light - invisible radiation or light that burns skin

INDEX